WORLD CUP ACTION!

BY
BILL GUTMAN

WATERMILL PRESS

Library of Congress Cataloging-in-Publication Data

Gutman, Bill.
World cup action! / by Bill Gutman
p.   cm.
ISBN 0-8167-3376-7
1. World Cup (Soccer)—History—Juvenile literature.
[1. World Cup (Soccer)—History. 2. Soccer—History.]   I. Title.
GV943.49.G88 1994
796.334'668—dc20   93-41721

Printed in U.S.A.

10 9 8 7 6 5 4 3 2 1

Cover photo © 1994 Allsport/D. Strohmeyer
All interior photos © 1994 Allsport except p. 23, © 1994 Time Inc.

INTRODUCTION

It is, by far, the most popular sport in the world. In most places it's called *football*. In the United States and Canada, however, the game is called *soccer,* so that it isn't mixed up with American football. And from June 17 through July 17, 1994, the United States will host the World Cup, the premier soccer event and largest sporting event in the world!

The worldwide popularity of soccer is mind-boggling. Modern soccer began in England in 1863. The English helped spread the sport to many other countries. In 1904, FIFA was formed. FIFA stands for Fédération Internationale de Football Association (International Federation of Association Football in

U.S.A. WELCOMES WORLD CUP SOCCER "94"

Allsport/David Cannon

The World Cup is coming to America in 1994. This "Uncle Sam" reminder was at a U.S. Cup match in 1993. By now, all soccer fans know just where the famed Cup matches will take place.

English). This organization governs soccer in more than 170 countries. By 1908, soccer had become an Olympic sport, and in 1930 the World Cup tournament took place for the first time.

Interest in soccer has grown more slowly in the United States. That's because Americans always had baseball, football, and basketball to play and watch. But today there are more than 15 million people playing soccer in the United States. That's 23 percent more than played in 1987! Of these, 11.6 million players are under the age of 18. As the U.S. National Team continues to do well in competitions, interest is growing quickly among older Americans, too.

Allsport/Shaun Botterill

The United States' Mike Lapper goes high in the air to head the ball away from his Saudi Arabian rival during play in the International Cup tournament in 1992.

WHAT IS THE WORLD CUP?

The World Cup is the greatest trophy in soccer. The national teams of all soccer-playing countries have a chance to win it. There is a great deal of national pride at stake. Each country wants to win the Cup and be able to say that its soccer team is the best in the world!

Because the World Cup tournament is so important, it is held only once every four years. That gives each country a chance to get its best players together for its national team. Because so many countries want to play for the Cup, it takes nearly two years to play all the qualifying games.

Only 24 of the over 170 national teams that belong to FIFA can play for the World Cup. Of these 24, the team that won the World Cup the last time it was played and the team from the country where the tournament is being played that year qualify automatically. Those two teams for the 1994 World Cup are Germany and the United States. The other 22 teams must win a series of games to qualify.

When the first World Cup was played in 1930, only 13 countries entered the tournament. It was played in Montevideo, Uruguay, in Central America. Uruguay won the championship to the delight of its fans. Since then, the tournament has been played every four years. It wasn't played in 1942 and 1946 because of World War II.

Brazil, Germany (formerly West Germany), and Italy have won the Cup three times each. Uruguay and Argentina have won it twice. A complete list of World Cup winners, head coaches, and the runners-up is on page 5.

Kempes of Argentina throws his hands up in jubilation after scoring a goal in the 1982 final against the Netherlands. The paper littering the field shows the Argentine fans were overjoyed as well.

Allsport

QUICK FACT

If past World Cup history is a guide, the United States team has a very good chance to reach the final game in 1994. In 14 previous World Cups, the host country has won five times and been runner-up twice. That means in one-half of the tournaments, the host country has reached the final game. Good odds!

England's great Bobby Moore holds the Cup aloft after his team won in 1966 before its home fans.

Allsport

Year	Host Country	Champion	Head Coach	Runner-up
1930	Uruguay	Uruguay	Alberto Supicci	Argentina
1934	Italy	Italy	Vittorio Pozzo	Czechoslovakia
1938	France	Italy	Vittorio Pozzo	Hungary
1950	Brazil	Uruguay	Juan Lopez	Brazil
1954	Switzerland	West Germany	Sepp Herberger	Hungary
1958	Sweden	Brazil	Vicente Feola	Sweden
1962	Chile	Brazil	Aymore Moreira	Czechoslovakia
1966	England	England	Alf Ramsey	West Germany
1970	Mexico	Brazil	Mario Zagalo	Italy
1974	West Germany	West Germany	Helmut Schoen	Netherlands
1978	Argentina	Argentina	Cesar Menotti	Netherlands
1982	Spain	Italy	Enzo Bearzot	West Germany
1986	Mexico	Argentina	Carlos Bilardo	West Germany
1990	Italy	West Germany	Franz Beckenbauer	Argentina
1994	United States	?	?	?

THE 1994 WORLD CUP

How To Qualify

One hundred forty-one countries started out with the hope of winning the 1994 World Cup. Defending champion Germany (formerly West Germany) and the host country United States do not have to play qualifying matches. By November, 1993, the 141 countries played some 500 matches. From these matches will come the 22 other teams to qualify for the 1994 tournament.

The qualifying matches are played in six zones called **Confederations**. They are:

1. CONCACAF — North & Central America & the Caribbean
2. Oceania (Australia)
3. Asia
4. Africa
5. South America
6. Europe

Niall Quinn and Paul McGrath of Ireland both try to get the ball past Denmark's goalkeeper Peter Schmeichel during World Cup qualifying action in 1993. The game ended in a 1-1 tie.

Norway's goalkeeper Eric Thorsvedt tumbles to the ground while trying to stop a shot by England's Les Ferdinand. This was Thorsvedt's day as he and his teammates won the qualifier, 2-0.

Arms, legs, and heads are all flying as players from Ireland and Denmark battle during World Cup qualifying action.

Who said soccer is a non-contact sport? Arsene Hobou of the Ivory Coast takes a tumble as Algeria's Abdelhafin Tasfaout goes after the ball during this battle to qualify for the World Cup.

The different countries must qualify within their own zone. But to qualify, some teams must beat teams from other zones, too. Here are some quick examples of how qualifying works in each zone.

1. CONCACAF — Two or three teams will be in the finals. This includes the United States as host country. The other teams must play each other. The winner of the first round of play qualifies. The runner-up can also qualify but must win another playoff round against teams from Oceania and South America to keep its Cup hopes alive.

Allsport/Simon Bruty

2. Oceania — Only one team can qualify, but it must win a playoff against teams from CONCACAF and South America to get a berth in the final 24-team field.

3. Asia — There will be two teams that qualify from the 28 that started. The 28 teams are divided into six groups with group winners advancing to a second round of play. The winner and runner-up from the second round will qualify for the Cup.

4. Africa — Nine first-round group winners will be put in three second-round groups of three teams each. The winners of each of the three groups will qualify.

Allsport/Shaun Botterill

Speed is one of the elements that make soccer so exciting. World-class players can control the ball while running at full speed.

5. South America — Three or four teams will qualify. There are nine countries entering play. They play in two groups — one of five teams, the other of four. The winner and runner-up from the five-team group qualify. The winner of the four-team group also qualifies for final Cup competition. The runner-up from the four-team group plays the winner of the Oceania/CONCACAF playoff to pick yet another qualifier.

6. Europe — There will be 13 teams qualifying from this largest zone. The 36 countries are divided into six groups. Each group plays a "league" playoff, with the top two teams from each group qualifying for the Cup. The 13th European team is defending champ Germany (formerly West Germany).

That's how the final 24 teams are picked. It's a long, hard grind to find the best teams. But the reward can be great. It's the dream of every player on every team to hold the World Cup trophy proudly aloft. But the real work has just begun. Even though these world-class teams have come through two years of qualifying competitions, they still have to face each other in the 52 World Cup matches!

Garcia Aspe (number 8) of Mexico executes a perfect fake as he prepares to take the ball to his right. Notice how the El Salvador defender is leaning the wrong way.

Allsport/David Leah

9

THE WORLD CUP SCHEDULE

The 24 teams competing for the 1994 World Cup will play a total of 52 games. In the first round, the teams will be divided into six groups of four teams each. Six teams will be determined to be the top "seeds" and will be placed as the top team in each group. The others will be placed by a random "draw."

The groups will be named by letter — A, B, C, D, E, F.

There will be 36 games in the first round. Each team will play the other teams in its group, earning three points for a win, one for a tie, and none for a loss. The top two teams from each group (12 teams) will qualify for the "Round of 16." The four best third-place teams will also qualify.

At this point, the tournament becomes single-elimination. One defeat and a team is out. If any game at this point is tied after regulation play (two 45-minute halves), there will be a 30-minute overtime. If there is still no winner, then penalty kicks will be taken to produce a winner.

The eight winners will then play quarterfinal matches to determine the four semifinalists. The two semifinal games will then produce the two remaining teams that will play the final match for the World Cup. The semifinal losers will play a match for third place.

THE TROPHY

The original World Cup trophy was a solid gold cup designed by the French sculptor Abel LaFleur. It was named after Jules Rimet. Rimet was the president of FIFA from 1921 to 1954, and he played a major role in organizing the first World Cup competition. This trophy was given to Brazil after their third World Cup victory in 1970.

The present World Cup trophy is 14 inches (36 cm) tall and weighs 11 pounds (4.97 kg). It is made from 18 carat solid gold and was designed by Italian sculptor Silvio Gazzaniga for the 1974 tournament. The top of the trophy has a replica of the world and below it rise the figures of two athletes at the moment of triumph. It is the most sought-after trophy in the world.

Allsport/Shaun Botterill

This is what it's all about, the ultimate goal of all soccer players everywhere. The World Cup trophy is not only a beautiful gold sculpture, but winning it means your country's national team is the absolute best in the world.

Allsport/David Leah

Argentina's great star Diego Maradona led his country to the championship in 1986.

Stanford Stadium

After the United States was chosen to be the host country for World Cup 1994, as many as 32 cities from Honolulu to Boston wanted to host the matches. Nine sites were finally chosen for the June 17-July 17, 1994 tournament. See if there is one near you.

1. Foxboro Stadium in Boston, Massachusetts — Capacity: 61,000 fans. First-round World Cup games will be played at Foxboro on June 21, 23, 25, and 30. A game in the "Round of 16" will be played here on July

Pontiac Silverdome, the first indoor stadium to host a World Cup event.

5, and a quarterfinal game will be held on July 9.

2. Soldier Field in Chicago, Illinois — Capacity: 66,814 fans. First-round World Cup games will be played here on June 17, 21, 26, and 27. A "Round of 16" game will be played on July 2.

3. The Cotton Bowl in Dallas, Texas — Capacity: 72,000 fans. First-round World Cup games will be played here on June 17, 21, 27, and 30. A "Round of 16" game is scheduled for July 3, and a quarterfinal contest for July 9.

4. The Pontiac Silverdome in Pontiac, Michigan — Capacity: 76,000 fans. The Silverdome will be the first indoor, domed stadium to ever host a World Cup game. First-round World Cup games are scheduled for June 18, 22, 24, and 28.

5. The Rose Bowl in Pasadena, California — Capacity: 102,083 fans. First-round World Cup matches will be played June 18, 19, 22, and 26. A "Round of 16" contest will be held July 3; a semifinal game on July 13; the match for third and fourth place on July 16. On July 17, 1994,

the Rose Bowl will be the site of the World Cup championship game.

6. Giants Stadium in East Rutherford, New Jersey — Capacity: 76,891 fans. First-round World Cup action will be held here on June 18, 23, 25, and 28. A "Round of 16" match is set for July 5; a quarterfinal contest for July 10; and a big semifinal game on July 13, 1994.

7. Citrus Bowl in Orlando, Florida — Capacity: 70,188 fans. The stadium will host first-round World Cup games on June 19, 24, 25, and 29. A "Round of 16" match will be played on July 4.

8. Stanford Stadium in Palo Alto, California — Capacity: 86,019 fans. Stanford Stadium will host first-round World Cup games on June 20, 24, 26, and 28; a "Round of 16" match on July 4; and a quarterfinal game on July 10.

9. Robert F. Kennedy Memorial Stadium in Washington, D.C. — Capacity: 56,500 fans. First-round World Cup games are scheduled for June 19, 20, 28, and 29. A "Round of 16" match is set for July 2.

MEDIA COVERAGE

There will be incredible worldwide media coverage of the 1994 World Cup. In the United States, all 52 games will be on television. It is estimated that as many as 31.2 billion people worldwide will watch the 52 World Cup matches on television via satellite. The final game could be watched by as many as 2 billion people!

In 1986, 652 million watched the final, and in 1990, 1.06 billion saw Germany (formerly West Germany) win the Cup. The 1994 audience may be twice that!

By comparison, some 253.4 million fans worldwide watched the 1993 Super Bowl Game between the Dallas Cowboys and Buffalo Bills. That's why the World Cup is still considered the largest single-sport event in the world!

The Rose Bowl, where the 1994 World Cup championship game will be played.

13

THE UNITED STATES NATIONAL TEAM

Allsport/David Leah

Members of the United States National Team line up before the start of the 1993 Gold Cup match.

The United States has been playing international soccer for a long time. The U.S. Soccer Federation has been a member of FIFA since 1913. Team USA competed for the first World Cup in 1930. The team returned again in 1934 and again in 1950. But the United States has never real-ly been a world power in soccer.

In fact, after 1950 it took another 40 years before Team USA made it through the qualifying rounds and played for another World Cup.

Playing in Italy in the 1990 finals, the United States lost three straight games to be eliminated.

But they lost by only a 1-0 score to host Italy and then 2-1 to Austria. It was a good team that was definite-ly world class. That gave soccer fans around the United States high hopes for 1994, especially since the U.S. would be the host country!

THE MISSION VIEJO TRAINING CENTER

Allsport/Al Bello

With soccer growing in the United States and the National Team getting better, it was decided that the team needed a permanent training facility. That way, the National Team could train every day. The site that was chosen is in Mission Viejo, California. It opened on Jan. 11, 1993.

"I've been to Brazil, Italy, and many other countries," said United States goalkeeper Tony Meola. "This is the best facility of them all." It is a beautiful training facility, located about 50 miles (80.5 km) south of downtown Los Angeles. There are two full-size, lighted soccer fields and a 3,800 square foot (342 sq. m) clubhouse. The facility is on seven acres (2.8 hectares) of land and cost $3.3 million to build. Since the site opened, the U.S. National Team has trained twice a day, six days a week. Like all the other soccer-playing countries in the world, their goal is to win the World Cup in 1994.

Practice sessions for the U.S. National Team are sometimes grueling. The players must be in top form, both physically and mentally, to meet world-class players from other countries.

The U.S. National Team often trains by running in the deep sand by the ocean. And if you think running on sand is easy, just try it for a while!

Allsport/Simon Bruty

THE PLAYERS

The youngest player on the 1990 World Cup team, Chris Henderson, gets better every year. A midfielder, Henderson comes from a soccer-playing family and his goal ever since he was a youngster has been to win the World Cup.

The United States National Team will be selected from a pool of about 36 players. Most of them have a good deal of international experience. By the time the World Cup begins the players will range in age from 20 to 37. A number have played in top leagues overseas, while some have come from United States college programs.

Roughly one-third of the players are foreign-born, though all now live in the United States. Among the most experienced and well-known are defensemen Marcelo Balboa, Paul Caligiuri, and Fernando Clavijo; midfielders John Harkes, Chris Henderson, Dominic Kinnear, Bruce Murray, and Hugo Perez; forwards Peter Vermes and Eric Wynalda; and goalkeeper Tony Meola.

The coaches will pick the final World Cup squad from the player pool shortly before the tournament begins. They will base their decision on the players' skills, their health at the time, and the way the individuals blend with each other to form a team. That is the key. As with other sports, it's the chemistry between the players that's most important. For only a true "team" can win the World Cup.

Allsport/Shaun Botterill

Roy Wegerle (right) is a relative newcomer to the National Team. A star in England, he became a United States citizen in 1991 and now wants to help his adopted country win the World Cup. Wegerle scraps for the ball against England in a 1993 U.S. Cup game that the USA won.

Midfielder Bruce Murray is the USA's all-time leader in full international appearances and goals. Here he battles for the ball in a 1992 game against Italy.

Goalkeeper Tony Meola has been playing international soccer since 1988, when he was 19 years old. He was the goalie on the 1990 United States World Cup team and hopes to help lead the '94 team to soccer's greatest prize.

AN AMERICAN IN ENGLAND

A superstar in both England and America, John Harkes plays every game the same way—hard and to win.

John Harkes is a member of the U.S. National Team player pool. The 5'11" (1.81 m), 165-pound (75-kg) midfielder has a good chance of playing with the United States for the World Cup. He is the first American to become a superstar in one of England's toughest leagues.

Born in Kearny, New Jersey, on March 8, 1967, soccer was John's favorite sport at an early age. He became a star player at the University of Virginia, then joined the U.S. National Team in 1987 at the age of 20. Harkes played for the United States in the 1990 World Cup and was the Most Valuable Player in U.S. Cup '92.

He began playing for Sheffield Wednesday in England in 1990. In December of that year he scored the English League's Goal of the Year when he blasted a 35-foot (10.67-m) shot past one of England's greatest goalkeepers. Then in April of 1993, he became the first American to score a goal in the Coca-Cola League Cup Final at Wembley Stadium before 80,000 fans. And a month later, he became the first American to play in the F.A. Cup final in England.

John Harkes is surely an American soccer pioneer. Now perhaps he will help his native country win the World Cup!

On the soccer field, Harkes has quickness and tenacity. He also has that special quality all the great ones have, the ability to make the big play.

THE COACHES

Allsport/Shaun Botterill

To produce a world-class soccer team, it's important to have a top-notch coaching staff. The head coach of the U.S. National Team is Bora Milutinovic. He is known in the soccer world simply as "Bora." Born in Yugoslavia, Bora now calls Laguna Niguel, California his home. He has been the head coach of the U.S. National Team since March 1991.

Before managing the United States Team, Bora led both Mexico and Costa Rica into the World Cup final tournaments in 1986 and 1990. He was also well-known as a player throughout Europe in his younger days. Asked why America can become a great soccer power, Bora says, "The North American player is an athlete with extraordinary qualities, such as the ability to play hard during an entire match. The United States player is capable of learning very quickly. Therefore, teaching is easy."

Bora's assistant coaches are Timo Liekoski, Steve Sampson, and Sigi Schmid.

Bora is an intense, dedicated teacher. When he talks to National Team members, they listen.

THE CANADIAN TEAM

Canada entered World Cup competition for the first time in 1957. The team defeated the United States team twice in the early rounds but did not qualify for the 1958 Cup finals. The Canadians have fielded a World Cup team ever since. They qualified for the final tournament only once, in 1986. But they continue to get better.

Several players on the National Team have starred in top leagues in Europe. Goalkeeper Craig Forrest; defensemen Frank Yallop, Randy Samuel, Colin Miller, and Paul Fenwick; forwards Alex Bunbury, Paul Peschisolido, and Geoff Aunger; and midfielder John Limniatis all played in Europe before World Cup '94 qualifying action began.

Bob Lenarduzzi has been the head coach of the Canadian National Team since February 1992. Lenarduzzi played with the 1986 Canadian World Cup team, and he hopes to make the Canadians a world power in soccer. Under Coach Lenarduzzi, the team has risen from 66th to 46th in the world rankings.

The Canadian National Team came painfully close to making the 1994 World Cup final tournament. In the two rounds of the CONCA-CAF qualifying matches, Canada won five, lost three, and tied four. In the final round, their record was 3-2-1, and they finished second to Mexico. This meant that Mexico automatically qualified for the World Cup finals, and Canada had to play Australia in a playoff match.

A sellout crowd at Edmonton's Commonwealth Stadium watched Canada win the first game, 2-1, on July 31, 1993. Then on August 15, Australia won the second game, also by a 2-1 score. Since the total numbers of goals scored in the two games would determine the winner, and since each team had scored the same number of goals, the tie was decided by penalty kicks. Australia won the penalty kick shootout, 4-1, and Canada was eliminated.

Canada had played 14 qualifying games, more than any other nation seeking a World Cup final spot. The team just missed qualifying, but it was an exciting year for Canadian soccer.

Canada's Mario Rizi (in red) fights for the ball against a pair of Mexican opponents. Unfortunately, the Canadian team failed to qualify for the Cup finals in 1994.

Allsport/David Leah

Dale Mitchell of Canada goes airborne as he attempts to start an attacking sequence against Mexico.

THE LEGEND OF PELÉ

In every sport, there are a few special players who always seem larger than life. They remain that way even after they retire. With soccer, the man who stands far above all others is Pelé. His name is still magic all over the world.

Pelé's real name is Edson Arantes do Nascimento. Pelé was a nickname his friends gave him as a youngster. He didn't like it as first. Now he sure does. Pelé was born in Três Coracòes, Brazil, on October 23, 1940. He became a professional with the Santos Football Club at age 15. Two years later, in 1958, he led the Brazilian National Team to the World Cup. He was also a member of World Cup title teams in 1962 and 1970.

Pelé also helped soccer in the United States. He joined the New York Cosmos of the North American Soccer League in 1975. With Pelé in the line-up, Cosmos attendance went from 5,000 a game to more than 60,000 a game. He was the NASL Most Valuable Player in 1976 and retired after the 1977 season at the age of 37. After Pelé retired, many people slowly lost interest in the league and it was disbanded in 1985.

During his career, Pelé scored 1,281 goals in 1,363 games. He had 93 hat tricks (three goals in a game), scored four goals 31 times, six goals five times, and once scored an amazing eight goals in a single game! Today, Pelé is still the best ambassador soccer has. He is loved and respected everywhere, and continues to work hard to make the sport he loves even better.

Pelé. His name is the most magical of all.

In July 1971, the great Pelé played his last game with the Brazilian National Team. More than 120,000 fans chanted, "Stay! Stay! Stay!" to the man who had led his country to three World Cups.

THE FANS

The World Cup qualifying matches include teams from all over the world. And wherever a national team goes, its fans can't be far behind. Soccer fans are among the most vocal and colorful of any sport.

As the United States becomes a world-class soccer power, more American flags can be seen at Team USA's matches.

occer fans love their teams with a passion not often seen in other sports. And nothing excites soccer fans more than the World Cup. Every fan in each country wants their national team to first qualify, then win the World Cup. That's why each World Cup qualifying match has fans rooting wildly from the opening whistle.

Not only do the fans come to root for their teams; they also come to show great pride in their countries. During a World Cup year, fans often come to the matches dressed in tradition-

al native costumes. They sometimes paint their faces and bring flags and streamers. The colors in the stands at World Cup matches are often spectacular!

The small country of Uruguay won the first World Cup in 1930. Its fans are no less excited today.

KIDS & SOCCER

Soccer and kids make a perfect match. Of all the major sports, soccer is perhaps the most fun and healthiest for kids to learn. They can start at almost any age. All it takes to play is a ball and a couple of friends to practice the skills.

Soccer teams are well-organized for all age levels around the world. Everyone

playing the game. And it's a great game for girls as well as boys. Just look at these photos. The kids playing here aren't only having fun; they're working hard, and they're good! Someday, some of them might play for the World Cup.

It's obvious these youngsters know how to play the game. Early training teaches the basic skills. Then, it's a matter of practice, practice, practice. And it's fun, too.

Soccer is a game that can be played almost anywhere. These kids from Senegal in Africa don't need uniforms or a crowd to enjoy a quick game in an open clearing.

gets to play and get into good physical condition because of the nonstop action and running. In addition, playing soccer teaches the values of teamwork, responsibility, and good sportsmanship.

Kids all around the world take soccer very seriously. Even in the United States, where soccer is not a major professional sport, more kids than ever are

Soccer is a great sport for young girls as well as boys. It's good, healthy fun and with each passing year more girls are playing in leagues at every age level.

25

FABULOUS WORLD CUP FACTS AND FEATS

Pickles to the Rescue

The original World Cup trophy had a strange odyssey. It was hidden under a bed in Italy during World War II so it wouldn't be stolen. But it *was* stolen in London, England just before the 1966 World Cup final. The police couldn't find it. But a mongrel dog named Pickles did. He found the valuable prize buried under a garden hedge, making Pickles a hero in the soccer world. The cup was eventually presented to the Brazilian team after their third World Cup victory in 1970. It was then stolen from its display area in Rio, and has not been seen since.

Allsport/Steve Morton

Who Needs the Cup?

Today, the World Cup is the most prestigious sporting trophy in the world. But it wasn't quite that way when it began in 1930. Countries such as Austria, Germany, Hungary, and Switzerland refused to send teams to compete for that first ever trophy. The reason: They felt the sea voyage to Uruguay was too costly!

If He Only Had Shoes

Brazil's 6-5 victory over Poland during the 1938 World Cup is still considered one of the greatest matches in soccer history. The star was a Brazilian center forward named Leonidas da Silva, who scored four goals. What made it even more amazing was that Leonidas romped up and down the field all afternoon in his bare feet!

Allsport/David Cannon

Brian Laudrup of Denmark leaps over a tackle during a qualifying match against Ireland.

The First Hat Trick

There have been many great players from all over the world who have played their best in the World Cup. Yet the first player to ever score a "hat trick" (three goals) in a World Cup game was an Argentine. Guillermo Stabile scored his "hat trick" on July 19, 1930 as the Argentine team defeated Mexico, 6-3.

Scoring Machine

When Brazil won its second World Cup in 1958, the soccer world also got its first real look at the great Pelé. But it was a Frenchman named Just Fontaine who set a World Cup record that still stands. In six games, Fontaine scored an amazing total of 13 goals, an average of slightly more than two goals a game!

Read that Card

World Cup play had become so rough and brutal by 1966 that changes had to be made. One problem was that the players and the referees often spoke different languages. So in 1970, referees were given two different-colored cards. If a player saw the ref flash a yellow card to him, it was a warning. *Stop fouling.* If he didn't listen, he was shown a red card. That message was simple. *Get off the field. You're out of the game.* Everyone understood that!

Mexican defenders (in green) set up a human wall in front of their goal as Canadian attackers blast away during World Cup qualifying action in 1993.

Record Celebration

Argentina hosted the 1978 World Cup tournament. Despite a country filled with poverty, the government spent $700 million to build three new stadiums and fix up three older ones. Then in a case of the best possible finish, the Argentine team won the Cup. That set off a wild celebration around the entire country that lasted for days.

The Shot Heard Around the World

Some fans still call it the biggest goal in U.S. soccer history. It happened on November 19, 1989. Paul Caligiuri of the U.S. National Team sent a dipping 35-yard (31.85-m) shot past the Trinidad & Tobago goalkeeper to give the United States a 1-0 victory. More importantly, the win assured the United States a spot in the 1990 World Cup finals. It would be the first U.S. appearance in the finals in 40 years, signaling the return of the United States as a world-class soccer power. Caligiuri's goal is still referred to as "The Shot Heard Around the World."

Number One

Louis Laurent of France scored the first World Cup goal. It was on July 13, 1930 in a game against Mexico. France won the game, 4-1.

It's collision time for Ince of England and John Harkes of the United States during a U.S. Cup match in 1992. The United States won this game, 2-0, and continued to show everyone that they were now "world class."

An exciting moment between rivals Ireland and Northern Ireland as Ireland's goalkeeper Packie Bonner goes up high in a crowd to slap the ball away from Northern Ireland attackers.

Allsport/David Cannon

Oh, Baby!

The youngest person ever to play in the World Cup finals was Norman Whiteside. Whiteside was just 17 years, 42 days old when he played for Northern Ireland in a game against Yugoslavia on June 17, 1982. Until that time, Pelé was the youngest person to play in the Cup finals. The legendary superstar was 17 years, 237 days old when he played in 1958.

They Keep Coming Back for More

Brazil is the only team that has qualified for every World Cup final tournament. The Brazilians have won the Cup three times, an amazing soccer feat they share with Italy and Germany (formerly West Germany). Brazil was also given the honor of keeping the original Jules Rimet trophy after their third World Cup triumph in 1970.

Players and Head Coaches

There have only been two men who have played on a World Cup winning team and then coached teams that won the final match. Mario Zagalo played on the Brazilian teams that won the Cup in 1958 and 1962. He then coached Brazil in 1970, when the team emerged as World Cup winners for a third time.

Franz Beckenbauer was a star player with the West German team that won the World Cup in 1974. He later became head coach of the group that went on to victory in 1990.

Here is the list of the final 24 teams that will play in the 1994 World Cup:

Group 1

- **United States**
  (*host country*)
- **Germany**
  (*formerly West Germany, winner of the 1990 World Cup competition*)
- **Argentina**
- **Italy**
- **Brazil**
- **Belgium**

Group 2

- **Spain**
- **Russia**
- **Cameroon**
- **Ireland**
- **Romania**
- **Mexico**

Group 3

- **Colombia**
- **Netherlands**
- **Morocco**
- **Bulgaria**
- **South Korea**
- **Sweden**

Group 4

- **Bolivia**
- **Greece**
- **Nigeria**
- **Norway**
- **Saudi Arabia**
- **Switzerland**

WORLD CUP '94 SCORECARD

*F*ollow the action at home or at the matches with these fun scorecards.

Match:_____ Site:_____ Date:_____

Team #1: _____

Starting Players

Goalkeeper:_____

Defenders: _____

_____

Midfielders:_____

_____

Forwards: _____

_____

Substitutions:_____

_____

Goals Scored: _____

_____

Shots on Goal: _____

_____

Penalties: _____

_____

Match:_____ Site:_____ Date:_____

Team #2: _____

Starting Players

Goalkeeper:_____

Defenders: _____

_____

Midfielders:_____

_____

Forwards: _____

_____

Substitutions:_____

_____

Goals Scored: _____

_____

Shots on Goal: _____

_____

Penalties: _____

_____